I Wanttt a Unicorn Frappe!!!

An angsty girly comedy

By Catherine Weingarten

LICENSING & PRODUCTION INQUIRIES
Uproar Theatrics, LLC.
hello@uproartheatrics.com | www.UproarTheatrics.com

CHARACTERS (1M, 4 W)

Jenny- 20s-ish, female, very optimistic, so excited about love as a concept, likes to arrange pinecones, engaged to Sebastian.

Mom- 50s, female, very excited about marriage, a bit neurotic, loves granola.

Darla- 30s, female, wedding planner, little bit basic.

Cassandra-20s- female, Jenny's BFF, a poet and kinda intense and spacey, she could look at coco puffs for hours.

One male actor in his 20s-30s plays:

Sebastian- 20s-ish, male, emotionally mysterious, likes looking at the rain ala that angsty Hilary Duff music video when she cried a lot and rain fell at her.

Prince- too hot for an age, male, out of a fairytale.

*The cast should be diverse.

SETTING
A generic coffeeshop in the Midwest, a boring house and also sexy sugar dream world

TIME
Nowwwww

PROP Note: throughout the play the cup sizes keep getting bigger until they no longer resemble actual coffee cups.

Note:
( )=When a line is in parentheses it means it is quieter, hushed, smaller than a normal line
Emoticons= inject the line with the spirit of the emoticon or just inject it at the end of the line

A Note on Format and Language
The reader will instantly notice the unique format of the script. The language eschews standard spelling, grammar, and line breaks, and all are deliberate personal choices of the writer and are done to emphasize character and emotional truth. The writer is influenced by e.e cummings and his unconventional spelling and punctuation, as well as how millennials use language and textspeak. She also includes emoticons in her script which actors should see as an additional nonverbal emotional beat or "button" at the end of a line.

1. I'm Wedding Planning Without My Hubby...But Everything's Fine!

> *(JENNY and DARLA are sitting in a Starbucks-like generic coffee shop drinking boring looking coffees. There is a sign in the background that says, "Try the New Unicorn Frappe Today! Only available for four days!")*

DARIA

So... Jennnny... DREAM wedding... paint it for meee???
Any last minute touches we can do?
Cinderella carriage? Candles? Babies carrying candles?
Actuallly
That sounds kinda dangerous... yet also interesting?
I'll write it down.
I'm sure you want some real Instagrammable moments.

JENNY

Yes, yes and YES!
So I want it to add some pink touches
Like pink cocktails,
Pink suits, like just such an adorable experience
You could die
And then we could have paramedics on hand in case that happens!

DARLA

Wow-wow-wow luvsss! Bold...

JENNY

Ahhh I still can't believe I'm engaged!!
And shall marry a real live man within
Nine months ahhh!

DARLA

Yayyy!!

(Awkward silence. They drink their coffees.)

JENNY
Ugh is it me or is this coffee wildly boring?

DARLA
It's just you hahah!

JENNY
Have you ever tried any of their frappes Darla?

DARLA
No, too many calories!
Oh um, I'm kinda on a radical diet
Where I watch episodes of Top Chef for thirty days straight
And like think about the food really intensely,
But not eat anything.

JENNY
Oh wow, intense….

DARLA
Uh huh.

(Weird silence.)

JENNY
You wanna hear the proposal story againnn?

DARLA
Of course.

JENNY

So Sebastian and I just had this intense
Five course meal
I paid for because
I have a job and stuff,
And we went to this two-dollar
Ice cream place
and he said he'd buy me
An ice-cream!
which was so kind of him,
And he got me
Mint chocolate chip ice-cream with gummy bears in it...
And he told me to be careful chewing,
Which was weird cause I'm a great chewer
And suddenly I felt something very hard
In ma mouth
And I realized I was not chewing on a gummy bear
But an engagement ring ahhh!
And then he pulled it from my mouth
And got on one knee
And said, "Jenny, will you marry me
And appreciate the joy of ice cream with me forever?
And I said... yesss

DARLA

Yasss! What a story!
It's getting to be crunch time
So really hope he'll start coming to our sessions again!

JENNY

Ya, of course!
He said he'd be here today...
So hopefully soon he'll show up!
He's been busy with SAT tutoring
And stuff
It's crazy, like there are so many kids who have like
No

JENNY (cont)
Chance of passing the SATS,
Like so many kids be dumb I guess…
But I can try.
God, I still can't believe I met him
Picking up a penny he dropped.
So romantic right??

DARLA

Oh yes!

JENNY

And he said
"Hi, my name is Sebastian ;)
That is my penny."
And I said,
"Hi, my name is Jenny.
I just love pennies so much,
Sorry I tried to acquire yours."
And then he handed the penny to me
And asked for my number.

DARLA

Wow, what a story! I love it!
Can't wait till I also have love ha ha ha :(
But I guess Sebastian's don't grow on trees???

JENNY

I'm sure you'll find someone too, Darla the wedding
planner!
Who can resist a wedding planner?
If you get engaged, your wedding will be so easy??
Very practical person to settle down with.

DARLA

haha oh stop!

JENNY

Ugh Sebastian,
Just wish so much he was here right now!
Did you know he's like sooo kind
Squirrels like cry being near him, like Snow White style?
And he can sometimes kinda snarky and likes to stay out late and
Work hard and has so many friends aka so popular
And to sum it up, like
He doesn't have normal characteristics,
More like the kinda characteristics you associate with a Ken doll
Aka the perfect man.

DARLA

What a pictureeee!

JENNY

Next time Darla I wanna bring
In my vision board.
That will be very beneficial for you.
It's legit so big like it takes up my whole bedroom wall
And it says things like "Happiness"
"I like happiness" "Don't dump your boyfriend"
"Love is the best thing" and "you look good in those shoes"
And there's like all these pics of us together-
Like some of the pics his face is turned away
Or he's blinking but no one ever said I was a master selfie taker
And like ugh you'd like it!
I put all this pink glitter on the poster board
So it like shimmers in the night
And so when he doesn't call or doesn't come home,
I look at the board and just touch the edges,
I just feel the hard specks of glitter under my fingertips
And it makes me feel like everything's gunna be ok,
Hee and if I'm drunk I sometimes try to lick it,

JENNY (cont)
But that's not really that good for you.

DARLA
Ya, I'd love to see it.
Let's try a word association game
To help us really focus on this wedding
And your goals for it-
Wedding

JENNY
Perfect

DARLA
husband

JENNY
Hot

DARLA
true love

JENNY
Relatable

DARLA
Flower girls

JENNY
Cute babies with good hair

DARLA
Marriage

JENNY
Dream goal

DARLA

Greattt! I always find that to be a good warmup,
Really connect to your gut feelings about this exciting event!

JENNY

I feel so connected.
I'm just so glad the applesauce factory
Where I work
Let me get extra hours off this month so we can meet so
often
Eee!

DARLA

Yes I love it!
Since our session is almost done, do you have any
Questions for me??

JENNY

Just one, the big one.
Oh Darla,
You've helped so many couples plan their big day,
How can you tell if they're gunna last forever
Or just like 5 days?

DARLA

Well
Are you happy when you look at him???
Does he appreciate your beautiful soul?
Does he find your body but "a wonderland"?
If you say yes to those three questions then you good, gurl!

JENNY

Well I said yes, to all three in ma head!
So that's good!
I'm getting married Darla! Eee!

You are!

2.I likey the Unicorn Frappe!

> *(JENNY sits with her BFF CASSANDRA at the
> coffee shop.)*

CASSANDRA

Ooo did you hear about these new unicorn frappes.
They just came out today!?
They're only available for four days
And they look very girly,
Like a little sexy pink volcano-
We should try!!
Yay and then I wanna hear about your wedding planning sesh
This morning!

JENNY

Um sure...
I love limited edition items wow!

> *(CASSANDRA leaves and comes back with two
> unicorn frappes.)*

JENNY

Wow, it's um...
I've never seen anything like it.
Woahhh woahhh it leaves me breathless

> *(JENNY starts drinking it intensely.)*

Omg the flavors, tastes like
Failed family vacations to Colonial Williamsburg

JENNY (cont)
And a sexy lucid dream.
Wowzzzz.

CASSANDRA
Wow ya a lot of flavorsss.

JENNY
It just tastes so happy
Like so many flavors in ma mouth
Like I've never really tasted the flavor "unicorn"
Like had a unicorn in my mouth
Is it weird I want to order anotherrrr?

CASSANDRA
Umm I don't know if that's such a good idea-
What about your wedding dress?

JENNY
I um won't eat anything else today!
You can really taste the unicorns you know,
It just makes me wanna smile all day long, all day
Longggg!
Do you feel it? The magic in your mouth?

CASSANDRA
Yaaa, totally woah!

JENNY
Ya, guess they're like a thing now.

CASSANDRA
So how's the wedding planning going?
It's getting so close now eeee!
You guys having fun?

JENNY

OMG so much fun,
Like I haven't seen Sebastian in a bit??
But I've been having fun!!

CASSANDRA

But you guys live together…

JENNY

It's just you know how he gets,
Like he's all 1900s and like
Disconnects from technology
And won't answer my twenty facetime calls but it's cool!
We really are all too connected
to technology anyway,
ригggght??

CASSANDRA

Wait so how long
has he not talked to you for??

JENNY

Like a week or so… but it's fine.
The wedding planning
Is like going so well
And like it's more about the bride than the groom
Anyway,
Like worse comes to worse he'll show up the day of and it'll
be fineee--

CASSANDRA

Like you are so nice and such a catch and like
Normal chicks aren't as kind as you.

JENNY

Aw thanks Cassandra!

CASSANDRA

Like why does he ignore your calls?
This is freaking me out…
Like that's not a thing.

JENNY

It's um sometimes a thing ok.
Like the human male is complicated.

CASSANDRA

You know if you want to back out of this,
It wouldn't be a big deal ok.

JENNY

It's ok to be jealous
Cassahhndra-

CASSANDRA

(You know I don't like it when you pronounce ma name like
that)

JENNY

THAT I'm Engageddd
And You're not!
It's like a big honor that I received…
And you didn't…
Like jealousy is so normal.

CASSANDRA

I'm not jealous ok.
Like I'm an artist and stuff-
Like I'm zen and stuff-like I'm beyond jealousy.
I just want you to be happy.

JENNY

Of course I'm happy!
I AM in love Cassandra!
Ever heard of it?

CASSANDRA

Umm ya...

JENNY

Like I'm so happy and stuff I can't handle it,
Like sometimes at night I legit can't sleep I just
Feel so much glee
Like I'm eating glitter or something and it's
Just filling up inside of me,
Like I could die right now, like
Cause I got everything I ever wanted and stuff,
Or like maybe die after the wedding,
Cause I want to experience that.

CASSANDRA

Well I'm glad you're feeling good about this.
LOL this drink is so sugary,
Like it's hurtin' my mouth.

JENNY

Please don't speak ill of the drink
Like in front of me.

CASSANDRA

It's kinda just a drink...but ok.
Um you think I could bring a last minute plus one to your
wedding?
Just didn't know what the protocol was
For your maid of honor.

JENNY

Oh yeah, you can totes bring one.

CASSANDRA

Oh yay!
Cause there's this hot dude at the gym
Whose like always sweating and stuff
And I just think he has so much wedding date potench.
Oo did you see that movie where like the hot chick is single
An like legit hires an escort to be her wedding date
And they they like legit have sex and she pays him
BUT THEN It turns out he loves her and they become a couple?
That movie is kinda weird yet also aspirational?

JENNY

Woot woot!

CASSANDRA

Well thanks again
Yet also (you probs shouldn't get married.)

JENNY

Have you ever just thought about love?
Like as a concept?
Like being just so so in love…
Like when you're in love…
Like everything the person says doesn't sound
Like words
They sound like peppermint sticks
And when you touch them
You feel like a fricking bomb exploded
Like it's scary yet hot,
And I just never felt that way before Sebastian,
And like when he says he doesn't wanna see me that much
Or that I suck at sex it doesn't matter
Cause like I have him, like I got this guy
This guy that makes me feel like
I'm perpetually on coke, but not

JENNY (cont)
In a dangerous way, and like nothing bad can happen
Cause he's there and his smile is like out of a wood cutting
Commercial
And like this is what I want for my life
I want to be with someone who makes me feel
Like I'm floating,
That makes me feel like a fairy princess
Like when he leaves the room, like
I can't breathe
Like I legit collapse, like I need
My inhaler shaped like his face,
Like I become paralyzed but then he comes back and
Like all is ok with the world,
Cause like we together,
Like I'm so lucky,
Like I got a guy who perpetually make me feel like
I'm eating an obese gingerbread house
And aren't I lucky??

> *(A PRINCE appears and crosses the stage and exits.)*

JENNY
Did you see that?? Omg it was so crazii

CASSANDRA
No…
I didn't see anything.

3.DO You Even Appreciate ma Unicorn Frappe?

> *(JENNY and SEBASTIAN have Unicorn frappes. Little bit of weird tension between them. A sign in the background says "Day Two of Unicorn*

Frappe! Get some Unicorn in Yo Mouth
Today!")

JENNY

This is like it's second day of existing-
So glad you're trying it.

SEBASTIAN

Wow, ya lotta sugar.
Cough

JENNY

Uh huh, ya I know, it's amazing.
I already had like three this morning…
So I uh met yesterday to go over stuff…
I thought you were gunna be there…

SEBASTIAN

Oo sorry I was at a wannabe lawyer's conference for a week
And just got out like a half hour ago
Forgot to tell you.

JENNY

That's ok!
It's ok, all good.
I'm so proud of you hun,
Trying to be a lawyer! Trying to better yourself!
You're going to be so hot and mean in court!

SEBASTIAN

Thanks Jenny!
But I am sorry I've been so crazy with work and stuff,
But chicks like doing that kind of stuff anyway right
Like planning??

JENNY

Yesss! We love it so much!
All planning all the time,
Even like planning what to have for lunch each day,
That's alotta fun
How was SAT tutoring??

SEBASTIAN

It was ok, tutored this one girl named Mildred,
Who like kept staring at me really intensely
And asking me if I wanted to have dinner
At her house with her family,
Like over and over and that was kinda distracting
To my lesson plan.
But I think she has SAT potential!

JENNY

Potential is important. Sometimes even better
Than just being good at something.
I love potential.

SEBASTIAN

Will you finish mine? I can't have anymore,
Ug I think it gave me a headache-
What's in this thing?

JENNY

I hope one day we'll live in a house
That's like too big to deal with,
Like fairytale big and it has like
A moat under it with like
Alligators and stuff and like deadly animals
Can you hold ma hand?

SEBASTIAN

It's um shaking a little.

JENNY

No, it's not.

SEBASTIAN

How many of these have you had?

JENNY

I forgot heeeeeeeee
Can you just go to the next session?
It's tomorrow
And I want to hear your wedding vision,
Darla wants to hear your wedding vision.
(I hope you don't leave again mysteriously.)

SEBASTIAN

I can try.

JENNY

Yay!! <3 <3 <3 <3 <3 !!!!!!

4. OMG What an exciting event is happening to me!

(JENNY is by herself at the coffee shop. It's late at night. She checks her phone. Suddenly PRINCE and unicorn appear.)

PRINCE

Hi Jenny.

JENNY

OMG what are you?

PRINCE

I'm a prince, Jenny. And this is my unicorn, Pecan Pie!
Don't be scared though, he's harmless.

JENNY

I thought I saw you before, but then
You disappeared.

PRINCE

Ya, that was me.
There were too many people around though.
I wanted to talk to you alone.

JENNY

Really?? Little old me?? Lil' ol' Jenny?

PRINCE

Ya, you've been drinking so many magical drinks,
You've summoned some magical energy in the universe
And now here I am.
Why are you here so late?

JENNY

I like couldn't sleep and stuff...
So like came here to like be closer
To the unicorn frappe.

PRINCE

Perfectly reasonable.
How's the wedding planning going with Sebastian?

JENNY

How do you know about Sebastian?

PRINCE

I know everything about you Jenny,
But not in a creepy way.
I just like am all knowing.
So how's the wedding planning going?

JENNY

I dunno… he keeps leaving town for mysterious reasons
And doesn't seem to want to help plan,
But that's ok right?
Like the bride should do it all anyway, right?

PRINCE

Don't couples usually plan it together though?
I wouldn't know though, I'm single.

JENNY

Wow, you're single…
And a prince.

PRINCE

Ya, I have so much money,
I like to stare at it sometimes

JENNY

Do you ever like swim in it? Music video style?
That sounds fun!

PRINCE

No, I haven't…
I should though!
That sounds like a great new hobby.
Do you partake in hobbies?

JENNY

Oh of course!
I love watching old movies,
Blowing bubbles and staring at my childhood
Dollhouse and seeing if it can teach me anything
About the nature of love and adulthood.

PRINCE

I love those hobbies.

                        JENNY

Thankee!
I like your unicorn.
So cute.

                        PRINCE

Thank you. I trained him myself.

                        JENNY

I'm scared I'm gunna have to plan
This whole wedding myself.
Like is it bad he sometimes won't talk to me or
Touch me or sometimes deletes my phone number
Or refuses to
walk my adorable pug Bobcake in public?

                        PRINCE

I don't know if those are good signs Jenny...

                        JENNY

Your unicorn feels so soft,
Like a daydream or something,
Like falling in love or something.
I'm jealous. I wish my dog was more mythical.
Like maybe if she had little hornn?? (KEWT)
I'd like her better then.
She would upset me less or bore me less.
You're easy to talk to.

                        PRINCE

Well that's part of the job,
We talk to commoners all the time.

                        JENNY

Sounds so glam.

*(PRINCE touches JENNY's face or does some
kind of bewitching sexy magical gesture and
JENNY is paralyzed in a hot way.)*

JENNY

Is it bad I like unicorn frappes so much?

PRINCE

It's not bad at all to like them.
They're meant to be liked,
They taste like a half off trip to Disneyland in yo mouth.
You should keep drinking them.

JENNY

Like I can't stop thinking about them.
Like I feel like I can feel every inch of my whole body
For the first time,
Like I'm just so awake.
Like before everything felt so grey,
Like so much wedding planning solo style
but suddenly
I'm all empowered and stuff
And my vision board has already gotten glitterier.

**5.Let's Plan Weddings but really I'll just think about
Unicorn Frappes!**

*(JENNY and DARLA sit at the coffee shop.
JENNY has a unicorn frappe and is noticeably
perkier. The sign now says, "Day Three of the
Unicorn Frappe! Don't Miss the Chance to
Ingest Magic Gurl!")*

DARLA

So let's talk about
cake!!
What kind would you like?

JENNY

Mmm something super sweet
Like uber sweet-like call your dentist on speed dial sweet
Cause you get a cavity from just being near it.

DARLA

Ok great!
That's super helpful.
Now we're a little behind on this one,
So we should pick one within the next day or so.
And what about Sebastian's prefs?
He's coming today right?

JENNY

He definitely is!
And you will love itttt!
Cause his ideas are like so good
He could have like his own TV show...
Where he like thinks about things
And tells them to an audience.
I didn't sleep much last night.
I'm not really sure what kinda cake he likes...

DARLA

Well that's ok,
Why don't you tell me more about
Your grandest cake dreams!
Think big Jenny-a gal only gets one wedding!

JENNY

Hmm well is there like a unicorn cake like
Made by a chic generic coffee shop taking over the world
like in conversation with the unicorn Frappe?
Like affiliated wit it?
Cause that would be nicee :)
I just think unicorns are so romantic ya know...
Cause love, love is so magical ya know
Like sometimes you can't even tell if it's real or not in yo
head,
Like if you're crazy or love made you crazy,
I can see this big like 50-pound unicorn cake
With like our faces on it but with little unicorn horns,
I think that would be adorbs.

(SEBASTIAN appears! yay!)

SEBASTIAN

Hey hon

JENNY

Hi I Love you <3 <3 <3 <3
I'm so happy you're here!

DARLA

Hi! My name is Darla, your wedding planner,
Nice to finally meet you...

SEBASTIAN

I'm sorry I'm a bit late...
Had this SAT tutoring fashion shoot
For our summer catalog.

JENNY

Ooo sexi sexi I want a copy!!!

DARLA

It's ok, no worries.
Just happy you're here.
Sebastian,
I hope to plan the wedding of both of your dreams!
I hope to make your fantasies into reality!
If you want a live mermaid, cloud machines,
Glitter wrestling, a live rap show, I'm your gal!

SEBASTIAN

That sounds great!
Well
what are we discussing today?

DARLA

Cake. I'm gunna get a list of the types of cakes
you guys like
And then next time we can taste them!

SEBASTIAN

Ok great.
This girl at SAT tutoring, Patti Cake, brought this biggg
Piece of chocolate chip banana cake
To tutoring today and whenever she got a wrong answer
She just attacked it,
Like ate the biggest piece, like calm it down gurlll
It's just the SAT.

JENNY

So weird.
I missed you so bad today…
You didn't answer any of my
Texts.

DARLA

So what kind of cake flavors do you like, Sebastian?

SEBASTIAN

I guesss, lemon? Maybe pineapple?

JENNY

Those were amazing answers.

SEBASTIAN

Thanks!

JENNY

Like too good of answers for you to be a man.

SEBASTIAN

Well I am, so…

DARLA

Well thanks for the answers.
We'll taste all those cakes
Next week!
Now Sebastian, Jenny and I already discussed this but I wanted
To hear from you,
Is there anything
about your upcoming wedding you're hoping for?
Is there any way I can make your wedding dreamsss
Come true
in a hot way?

SEBASTIAN

I was thinking it could be fun to have some wings served
During cocktail hour,
Help give the wedding
more of a manly Midwestern
feel
Like me.

DARLA
But one doesn't eat wings at a wedding... you eat petit fours
And candy marzipan shaped like a horse
or a wedding ring!

SEBASTIAN
Oh... sorry.

JENNY
Oh sweet Seb, lift up your face!
DO not be ashamed of your true needs!
Come on, ol' Darls, there must be SOMETHING!
We can do...
I want this wedding to reflect both of us...
Like both of us but mostly Seb,
Like I want it to reflect soo much of Seb it's a fricking mirror
Who could not want to go to a wedding that reflects him?
Like they would be so fucking lucky!

DARLA
Wow, uh no reason for foul language Jenny.
I will reflect on it ok you two?
I just have a certain rep to uphold,
Don't wanna be Instagram shamed... again

JENNY
Kkkkk

SEBASTIAN
I'm sorry if I'm messing things up.
I do want it to reflect
Me
but also both of us.

JENNY

That is the most romantic thing I've ever heard in my life,
Can you say it again and can you videotape it
Darla?

(DARLA takes out her phone to video it.)

SEBASTIAN(bad at film acting)
I'm sorry… if I'm messing things up. I do want it to reflect
Me but also both of us!!

(JENNY claps.)

JENNY

That was beautiful Seb,
Maybe a third career in acting for the cinema?
You know what,
I just feel so lucky to be here, to be part of this,
To be an almost married woman to this delightfulll
SAT tutor.

SEBASTIAN

I just want this wedding to have some rough edges,
Like some manly sections,
Like maybe some cage fighting during cocktail hour
Or like some live monkeys you can dance with
During the party,
Cause normal dancing is pretty boring,
And maybe like they can throw chocolates at people
While they dance
Cause that would be cool?
Yet kinda aggressive…
And maybe there could be periods when I just leave the
wedding,
Like me and all the groomsmen
And we just go to the local zoo and look around and like

SEBASTIAN (cont)

Maybe
Go to the next state and go antiquing or wrestling.
I just wanna have fun on my wedding day,
Is that too much to ask?
I just don't want it to be too girly, like a seventh grade
sleepover,
Like I want to be thought of,
I want to be thought of a lot.

JENNY

(I think about you so much.)

SEBASTIAN

And like maybe there could be cupcakes with my face on it
Like handed out throughout the day with like hearts
around ma face,
And like my self-esteem was just so lifted
I couldn't even handle it,
Like I'd never have to read another self-help book again
About hating my life or how to stop
Being aimless like a fricking plastic bag,
Like I'd just feel so good about myself I couldn't take it,
And I don't even think we need to do any vows,
Cause I'd rather just focus on the dancing and the eating
And the potential groom's trips to anotha state
And I think that'll make me happy.

DARLA

Veryyy creative ideas there... :/

JENNY

Wait, why don't you caree about the vows??
I think I need anotha unicorn frappe.

(JENNY gets an even bigger unicorn frappe.)

JENNY

Wow this one is so good,
Tastes like dreams and stuff,
Like taste-able dreams,
You should try some honey magic bear.

SEBASTIAN

Little too sugary for me, sry

JENNY

You should be sorry.

SEBASTIAN

You know I don't like too much sugar…
Upsets my stomach.

JENNY

Kk sorry, temporarily forgot.

DARLA

Let's chat gift bagsss!!

JENNY

Yessss! We love gift bags!
I think we'd like pics of us
As a couple
in it doing various activities
Such as prepping hot cocoa; post-hookup;
Snow shoeing; jumping off a cliff; and of courseee
Hot tubbin'
Would be such a sweet memento, so people would like
Remember our love.

SEBASTIAN

That sounds like alotta work to take all those pics,
What about a good old-fashioned keychain
With the wedding date

DARLA

Seb, I'm sorry to say this but that's a little
Bar-mitzvah-y,
You're not becoming a man, are you?
You're being married...

JENNY

Burn, wedding planner Darla!

DARLA

I just think at this instance,
Jenny's ideas are just better than yours.

SEBASTIAN

Whatever.

JENNY

Oh don't be sad Sebastian!
Don't be sad I'm so good at planning weddings
And you are intensely awful at it.
Oh please be merry Sebastian!
Seeing one tear from your eye, makes my heart break in
two--

SEBASTIAN

I'm not crying...

JENNY

So I was thinking I might sing my vows,
Would you both like to hear?

DARLA

Sounds delightful, pls do!

JENNY

Ohh Seb,
I love youuu,
From the right angle you kinda look like a Greek God,
Also you're the God of my heart,
I can't believe I met youuu,
I wanna drink your face like a Unicorn Frappe,
Which is a big compliment cause that is my new favorite
drink.
I hate myself but I like you and I think that's all that
matttersss
Let's get marrrrieddd!!

Dance break!!

> *(JENNY does an intense hip hop dance with*
> *some break dancing involved. SEBASTIAN and*
> *DARLA clap.)*

JENNY

I've been working on this whole routine for like two weeks
straight…
Like every night,
Could you tell?

SEBASTIAN

Course!

JENNY

Oh darn! Look at the time!
I actually have to head back to work.
So many people calling with questions
About apple sauce!
But this will give you two time to get acquainted
More!

DARLA

See you next session!

(JENNY leaves.)

DARLA

So you two…make a very…
Sweet(?) couple.
Have you dated many women?
You can be real with Darla, I'm your WEDDING planner!

SEBASTIAN

Yes I've um dated women…

DARLA

Well that's good to hear.

SEBASTIAN

Ugh to tell you the truth this whole wedding
Planning thing is stressing me out so much.

DARLA

Well it is very stressful,
Lucky for you it seems Jenny is taking the lead
With a lot of it.

SEBASTIAN

Well that is true.
Have you been wedding planning for a while Darla?

DARLA

Just ten years or so…
But that shouldn't reflect anything about my age haha

SEBASTIAN

I'm sure you are!
God I can't believe I'm getting married…
Like when I planned to have her choke on the ring
I hid in her ice cream,
I'm not sure how far in advanced I was planning…
Sorry if that sounds bad…
Moments like these I just think…
Banana.

DARLA

Good fruit…

SEBASTIAN

I mean that was her name.
My ex.

DARLA

Ohh interestinggg.

SEBASTIAN

When my ex Banana broke up with me
My heart melted into a thousand pieces,
Like I couldn't smile for a week.
She wasn't like that nice to me and would like
Repeatedly forget my middle name but it was ok,
Cause like
When we were together I felt alive
Like every atom in my body
Had become Valentine's Day themed pop rocks
And she used to like sew me clothing and watch
Me lift weights
And we'd just like do stuff together.
And then she dumped me for this dude
She hooked up with once,
Who works at Wendy's

SEBASTIAN (cont)

And I guess he would have been texting her while we were together
And giving her good discounts on fries
And just like that she was gone, no more Banana,
To this day I still can't eat a banana,
They just upset me. It's too much. Screw Potassium.
So like when I was trying to get over her
I would just lie on my couch and shove
Mac n cheese themed popcorn in my mouth
And watch "To Catch a Predator" and cry
And I thought I'd never feel anything again,
Like I'd be like numb or something forever,
That I'd just be drunk dialing Wendy's forever.

DARLA

And then you met Jenny right?

SEBASTIAN

Yup,
then one day I met Jenny
And she like asked me out and looked at me
Like I was a Renaissance sculpture come to life,
Like I changed her or something
Just by being hot,
And like everything I did just amazed her,
Like she'd take pics of me eating
At dinner cause she said my chewing
Was adorable
And then suddenly we were dating
And suddenly we were a couple
And suddenly this major life change happened
But I didn't even notice.
Wow, I'm sorry if that was too open.
And if this were a love story, I'd realize
I liked her more than Banana,
But I don't think this is a love story,

SEBASTIAN (cont)
I don't know what kind of story this is.

DARLA
It's ok.
Sometimes marriage comes upon you like a tidal wave
And you kinda just have to go with it.
I have lots of different clients in different
Kinds
Of relationships.

SEBASTIAN
That's comforting.

6.Mom, Drink a Unicorn Frappe wit me!

> *(JENNY and MOM sit in the coffee shop. The
> sign still says, "Day Three of the Unicorn
> Frappe! Don't Miss the Chance to Ingest Magic
> Gurl!"))*

MOM
Wow Jenny, I can't believe your wedding's only nine months
away!
I've been dreaming about this
Since you were a week old.

JENNY
Aw thanksss Mom! Ya, I'm really excited…
Have you tried the unicorn frappe yet?
It's this amazing girly unicorn flavored drink,
Today marks its third day of being alive.

MOM
Ugh I don't really like coffee…

JENNY

I still don't get that.
Everyone likes coffee…
My fricking pug Bobcake even likes coffee…

MOM

It just gets me all dizzy.

JENNY

Kkkk
Well I luvz it!!

MOM

Your father has been driving me crazy.
Sometimes I miss being single ya know,
Like taking long walks by myself or being allowed
To go out with friends
Or not having to get him dinner every night.
But you're gunna love love married life!
Love love love love love <3!
I remember before my wedding I was so
Nervous,
Like I couldn't even feel my body,
it legit felt like bubbles
and I was so happy and I just, I thought it would work out,
and I just knew I wasn't gunna be one of those women who
got divorced…
and I didn't, I never got divorced.
I remember trying on my wedding dress,
It had big puff cream sleeves
Like fricking marshmallow,
And I just tried it on over and over again
And I kept thinking:
What would he think when he saw me?
Would he cry?
Would he want to start a new life with me?
Would he wanna make a s'more out of me?

MOM (cont)
I hoped he would want all those things…
And more,
And no one can give you back that time,
That time when you think marriage is gunna be butterflies
And hugs and 1950s bliss,
No one can give you that back,
You just have to move forward and sometimes you realize
The one you're with thinks you're kinda dumb
Or is more interested in listening to himself
Than you
Or telling you what to wear,
But you'll be fineee, you'll totally be fine,
But don't drink too many of those frappes.
You'll be fine!
You excited for your honeymoon?

JENNY
Yaaa, Amish country is gunna be great!
So romantic yet historicalll.
We're gunna power down our phones
And just like make out while I wear a bonnet.

MOM
You sure you guys don't wanna go to
The Virgin Islands or something?

JENNY
We just both love history so much
And like riding buggies…
Mm this frappe is good

MOM
How many have you been drinking a day, honey?

JENNY
Just like one to seventeen or so….

MOM

You're gunna get fat Jenny, and that's gunna just be awful!
Who gets fat right before their wedding...
You're just ruining marriage
as an institution right now.

JENNY

It'll be fine.

MOM

Your Instagram the past two days is just
A pic of you drinking a unicorn frappe
Or hugging one...

JENNY

Touché...

MOM

Don't get fat Jenny!
You deserve better thingssss.

JENNY

I can try to stop...

MOM

Try ok!
Think about those wedding pics,
Think about them sitting in an album
In your future house
Foreverrr
And people looking at them for years and years.

JENNY

Visualizing

MOM

I think you're gunna look really pretty at your wedding
Jenny.

JENNY

Thanks Mom!
I'm so excited!!!!!!!!!!!!!!!!!!!!!!!!!
Eeep!
Oh Mother, what does it feel like to be married?
Does it hurt? Does it feel like going to the Seven-Eleven
drunk
At 1 am on a Monday?

MOM

No, I don't think so.
It's more like like
Sitting in a bathtub for too long, like and the water starts
To get coldd,
And the bubbles evaporate
And your rubber ducky hits you in the face by accident But
you shouldn't leave cause you said you were gunna take a
bath
Like you made a commitment to that bath!
So you stay, and it's cold...

JENNY

I. Love. Bubbles.

MOM

Well I love you!
Can't believe you're gunna get married...
Married to a man...
And not be with your dad and me anymore
(sometimes I wish you wouldn't get married
And just stay with me foreverrrr)

JENNY

Hunh??

MOM

Just so excited for you to move on with your life sweets!
You and Sebastian look so adorable together!
Like long lost siblings!

JENNY

Thanks mom! :)

**7.In my dreams, I like to drink Unicorn Frappes slowly
while I think about my future hubbs! I don't even mind
the brain freeze! It doesn't hurt too long and only makes
me wanna die a little!**

>*(JENNY and SEBASTIAN's home. JENNY calls
>CASSANDRA freaking.)*

JENNY

Hey, are you awake?

CASSANDRA

Ya, now I am…

JENNY

Did you know starting tomorrow the unicorn frappe
Will only be available for two more days?
Like it felt like such a long amount of time…
And now it's like nothing.

CASSANDRA

Everything's ok Jenny.

JENNY

maybe they'll bring it back?
Like cause of popular demand or something...
But maybe they won't.

CASSANDRA

I guess it's hard to tell.
Isn't Sebastian therr?

JENNY

No, he's out

CASSANDRA

Where is he?

JENNY

I dunno... probably trying to achieve his dreams
Or something.
Ugh I wish you were here.
Ugh I had this weird dream.

CASSANDRA

What was the dream about?

JENNY

I was like Sebastian and I were inside a unicorn frappe
Like swimming inside it
Like tasting it, like licking it, like floating
In it.
That was like
The good part.
But then Sebastian like
Started trying to smother me in the drink
Like choke me
And I like told him to stop but he didn't.
And then the drink started to look less pink and blue
And more like some

JENNY (cont)

Garbage themed drink
And then it became like a whirlpool
And like sucked me in
And I couldn't see anything anymore.

CASSANDRA

That sounds really scary Jenny,
But also cool?
Could I use some of that for a slam poem I'm working on?

JENNY

Yaaa

CASSANDRA

What's going on with you and Sebastian?
Do you think he doesn't love you or something?

JENNY

No um he probably does?
But he is gone all the time...
Sometimes I feel like I can't talk to anyone,
Like let them know how I'm feeling cause it'll just
freak them out.

CASSANDRA

Well you won't freak me out.
I once dated a dude who was a fisherman....

JENNY

I like that story.
How did you two break up again?

CASSANDRA

He cheated on me with a hot chick
Who cleaned boats
And called herself a modern day "mermaid"
Cause she didn't like to use her legs that much.

JENNY

That's a sad ending…
I don't like those.
It's just like
I feel like ever since I've been engaged
It's just something's been feeling weird
Like off.
But it's probably just jitters
Just cause it's soon soon ahhh.

CASSANDRA

I don't like how he's been treating you Jenny.
He should be there comforting you-
Throwing rose petals at your face
Every waking moments,
Baking you souffle
And serenading you when you wake up.

JENNY

Do men really do that?

CASSANDRA

Ya um…I'm sure.
That dream sounds dark though.
Maybe it's trying to tell you something?
Like that you two shouldn't get married.

JENNY

Dreams are rando.
Seb and I were made to be together,
I know that!
Like he proposed to me-like he chose me!
Can we not talk about him anymore?

CASSANDRA

kkkkkkk
Do you wanna come here and sleep?

JENNY

I think I'm ok…
Thanks though.
I'm gunna look really good in white, ya know?

CASSANDRA

Yaa
like too good.

JENNY

It's weird like in my head I keep
Seeing all these stars and stuff
And like unicorns and they're like friends and stuff
Like hangzin?
Sorry if I've been kinda overdramatic

CASSANDRA

Ya sounds super weird.

JENNY

I made a new vision board last night,
Like for my wedding,
It's like even biggerrr than my other vision board,
And it's white, aka bridal themed.
And I put some quotes on it that are wedding friendly like
"Wow, the bride is hot!" and "Till Death do us part,

JENNY (cont)

But don't ever die Sebastian cause I couldn't handle it"
And "Goal: get married"

CASSANDRA

Oo send pics!

JENNY

You know, we had this fight once,
He said I wasn't good in
The bedroom
He said I was boring,
So he was mad and I didn't know what to dooo,
Well behaved chicks aren't usually good in the bedroom,
We just smile a lot and try not to get too dirty
But he was just so mad at me,
But then we bought a sex self-help tape online,
And then it was a bit better.
I don't know why I'm telling you that story,
Maybe cause it was upsetting,
Cause like I hurttt him, like how could I do that?
Like I wasn't good enough and it was just awful
And I play it over and over again until
It's like a fricking screensaver in my mind.

CASSANDRA

Wait he said you were bad in bed?
That's so harsh.

JENNY

Or just really honest?

CASSANDRA

Or just douche central?
I no likey.

JENNY

I'm relly happy about this new vision board though!
Cause the other one was just about our relationship
And now our relationship is changinggg
And morphing
And I'm just trying to focus on our wedding,
I put some pics of our groomsmen and bridesmaids on it,
And a pic of his dead cat Sprinkles--

CASSANDRA

Wait like in da ground? Jennnyyyyy

JENNY

Not dead of course! Alive and vibranttt!
Living dat best life!
There's this cute pic
Of her when I threw her in the water ironically
And she was trying to bite my leg! Kewtt!
I know she's looking down on us and blessing our union.
I got tired.

CASSANDRA

Jenny, if you try to go to sleep
I can like listen and stuff...
Like make sure you do

JENNY

I'd like that.

8. Royalty is Hot but Not as Hot as me Drinking a Unicorn Frappe

> *(Late at night. JENNY is by herself at the coffee
> shop. The Prince appears without his unicorn.)*

PRINCE

Pecan Pie misses you.

JENNY

I missed him too.
And his edgy name.
You know you look kinda like him, in the right light.

PRINCE

I'm sure not. I have high-class genes.
He's from a poor,
peasant folk family.

JENNY

Sorry, didn't mean to insult you.

PRINCE

Let's go somewhere,
I want to go somewhere new!

JENNY

Ya um sure,
As long as you bring me back cause I have so many
wedding planning meetings,
Darla is very hands on.

PRINCE

It won't be for too long.
I want you to experience something special.
I want you to feel better.

> (JENNY and the PRINCE fly to a cloud.
> PRINCE has prepared a picnic for her.)

PRINCE

So this is a unicorn frappe sandwich
And a unicorn frappe apple
And unicorn frappe champagne.

JENNY

Mmm it looks so good!

PRINCE

I thought you'd likey.
You can be so much more creative than this
Basic unicorn drank.

JENNY

Please don't speak badly of the drink.

PRINCE

Kkkkkk

JENNY

I'm glad we're spending time together…

PRINCE

Ya it's kinda like a date…

JENNY

No guy's ever done something so nice for me.

PRINCE

Well that's sad.
How's wedding planning?

JENNY

Wedding planning is going well!
I'm really hoping
There's gunna be a unicorn cake for the wedding though,
Like with unicorn frappe icing in the middle.

PRINCE

I'm sure that cake exists.
If you believe in it
Hard enough.

JENNY

Thank you! You're so optimistic, I likey
That quality.
Not enough people believe in things.

PRINCE

That unicorn frappe looks good...
I wanna watch you drink it.

JENNY

Ya??

JENNY

Well I'm um engaged.
I probs shouldn't be doing erotic things for other men.

PRINCE

It doesn't count Jenny,
I promise.
Would he even care anyway?

JENNY

Ya, course he would care! He would care soo much,
Like so much caring he would throw himself
Off a building!
If he found out another man watched me drink a
High calorie fantastical themed beverage,
He would fricking get stuck in a water park slide out of sheer
Angst
And never come out,
Even if little babies hit him in the slide cause

JENNY (cont)

He was blocking it.

PRINCE

Feel like you're projecting.

JENNY

No projections, just truth.
Commitment is serious, love is serious.
I tattooed that to the back of ma head!

PRINCE

You're getting pretty pouty.

JENNY

I'm not being pouty!

PRINCE

I wanna kiss you so bad... I wanna kiss you
On ma unicornnn.

JENNY

Really??

PRINCE

You need to be transported Jenny,
you need to be treated bettterrr,
I can treat you so well, I can pamper you
Celebrity diva style,
I can sew you slippers with your face on it!
(I legit recently took a sewing class online)
I can bake you all the unicorn frappe cakes you want...
You don't need to get married to get a cake.
I can fricking make a unicorn bakery in your honor.
I bathe in rose petals and human tears.

                    JENNY

Into it.

                    PRINCE

I'm going to kiss you.

            (They kiss.)

                    JENNY

I wish this didn't count,
I wish you could just stop the world.

                    PRINCE.

It doesn't.
We stopped it,
It's just us now.

                    JENNY

Ack! I can't!
I I I
Don't know what I'm doing... I'm engaged to a
MAN.
Like we're a couple.
And I've never been in love like thattt,
No man has ever made me feel like thattt,
Like I'm not good enough to even be in the same
Room as Sebastian but he chose me.
I don't know what I'm doing.
Are clouds edible?

                    PRINCE

I don't think so...
Should I take you home?

                    JENNY

yaaaaa

9.OMG I might have done something bad, why isn't there Unicorn frappe themed vodka, I need it, wahh??

(JENNY and CASSANDRA at the coffee shop. A sign says, "Last Day of Unicorn Frappe ahhhh-Jenny will you be ok?")

CASSANDRA

I was thinking tomorrow night for your bachelorette party we could all go
To this glow in the dark sex shop
And then out for some drankssss.
Doesn't that sound fun?

JENNY

But isn't Quinn deathly allergic to glow in the dark stuff?

CASSANDRA

Whatevs, that's her problem.
It's yo wedding!

JENNY

Ya, you right! It is my wedding!
Suck it Quinn, have better genes!
Ya we can just have like a sexy ambulance on call
In case she collapses or whatevers.

CASSANDRA

Good thinking.
Uhhhhh
Being your maid of honor is so
FUN!

JENNY

Ya, ya totally.
Wow ma unicorn frappe, wow
tastes extra magical todayyy,
Like I can taste the fairytale ya know?

CASSANDRA

Sure…
I asked that hot dude from the gym out! He's so hot!
Like he could sell actual products cause of his
Hotness!
He said no though…
He said he's engaged
But at least I tried righttt?

JENNY

Ya just gunna say that!
That took guts!

CASSANDRA

Thanks Jenny :)

JENNY

Fuck, I need to tell you something.
But I can't!
But I should…
I'm not going to…
But maybe I shoulddd??

CASSANDRA

Tell moi!!

JENNY

I scared!!

CASSANDRA

Everything ok with Sebastian?
Did he change his phone number again
And not tell you?
I hateee
when he does that.

JENNY

I did something
Bad.

CASSANDRA

Did you steal something?
Cause just don't tell anyone ever about it,
Watevss,
I steal underwear from Victoria's Secret all the time
Cause sometimes they get in these cute blue underwear
With guinea pigs on them and I just find guinea pigs
Just so adorbs.
Doesn't affect anyone except
ma sex life.
Hee hee-

JENNY

I met someone else!

CASSANDRA

Waaaaaaaaaaaaaaaaaaaaaaaaaaaaaaaaaaaaaaaaaaaaaaaaaaaaaaaaaaaa
a

JENNY

I dunno, ahh,
I just felt really vulnerable and stuff
And I haven't seen Seb for a while
And this guy is just so nice and stuff
And kind of looks like him in the dark
And has a hot crown and his unicorn is (I'm serious)

JENNY (cont)

To die for!

CASSANDRA

A crown and a unicorn?
Jenny, it doesn't count if it's a
lucid dream/mental breakdown!

JENNY

No, it wasn't a dream! It was realll!
He was here, in this very generic coffee shop,
And he held me so tight
And he said I was perfect.
No guy has ever said I was perfect before :)

CASSANDRA

Uh huh…
And he was royal?

JENNY

Yaaaa.
I don't know what to do

CASSANDRA

Jenny, breathe deeply ok,
It's gunna be ok,
I legit think you're tripping on too many Unicorn frappes…
Like no one chick should drink this many,
Like you're not yourself,
You've gone to a sugar-ier place

JENNY

NO! I am in RE-AL-ITY!
You're in the sugar-ier placeee!
It's you!

CASSANDRA

Don't worry about this dude,
You probs just hallucinated him out of paranoia and fear
About your future,
Supa normal.
The mind is so weird.
I legit did a life-sized sculpture of the brain at school,
There were SO many sections,
Like it's so complicated.

JENNY

You know today is the last day of the unicorn frappe right?

CASSANDRA

What are you gunna do when they're goneee?

JENNY

I don't know...

CASSANDRA

You know you're kinda freaking me out Jenny
You just told me you were having an affair
With a Prince who had a unicorn....
I don't think you can handle these anymore.

(CASSANDRA takes JENNY's unicorn frappe.)

JENNY

Nooo waaaaaa what is WRONG WITH YOU!?
That drink has fricking magical propertiesss!
It's gunna be taken away tomorrow anyway.

*(JENNY starts licking the counter to see if she
can left over bits of unicorn frappe.)*

CASSANDRA

Ew stop licking that,
You're acting like a fricking New York orphan from the
40s…
Jenny, you are more than this drink!

JENNY

AM I? Am I really?

CASSANDRA

I feel like you're having all these feelings
But you just can't deal with them
So you're just drinking this ultra-sugary frappe.
Like I know planning a wedding is hard but maybe
It shouldn't be this hard?

JENNY

Like sometimes I wander if he even wants to marry me…

CASSANDRA

If your relationship was healthy
You wouldn't be having thoughts like that.

JENNY

But we're getting married,
Like it's an event that involves me.

CASSANDRA

Well maybe it shouldn't happen…

JENNY

Waaa you're my maid of honor…
Like dyou want your position revoked!!!

CASSANDRA

No…I like my position…

JENNY

Ugh I want ma unicorn frappe back!
It misses me!!!!
Don't take away ma BFFFFF!

CASSANDRA

What are these drinks filling in youuu?
Why do you need them so much?

JENNY

I dunno,
When I have them, the world becomes like
A Lucky Charms commercial and stuff,
Like so happy and I don't have to think about bad stuff,
Like not at all.

CASSANDRA

But the world isn't a Lucky Charms commercial...
It's like darker than that
And sometimes guys forget your name
Or make you crochet full outfits for them
And try to steal your sosh security code,
But that's just life,
And I'd like you to join me Jenny,
In this game of life!

JENNY

I can'ttttttt :(

> *(JENNY takes the unicorn frappe and pours
> some on CASSANDRA in rage and grabs
> another one and runs out intensely.)*

10. Oh Unicorn Frappe, why have you not manifested into cake form?

(At the coffee shop. MOM, JENNY, CASSANDRA and DARLA have cake in front of them.)

                    DARLA
Hi everyone, I'm Darla the wedding planner!
Thanks so much for coming to try some cake!

                    CASSANDRA
I'm Cassandra, the maid of honor and BFF to Jenny!

                    MOM
And I'm the mom!

                    JENNY
She's my mom!

                    DARLA
Wonderful!
So these three different kinds of cake are
from a feminist bakery close by called
"Second Wave of Yummy"
And are known for their sugariness.
They also prefer people
Ordering them closer to the wedding date
Because working in a shorter amount of time
Feels more feminist to them.

                    MOM
Sounds fun!

DARLA

All the ingredients are made
from feminist products.
So this flavor is Fuck the Patriarchy Vanilla,
This one is I Hate Men Matcha,
And this one is Weddings Are an Institution that Oppresses
Women
Lemon.

MOM

Hmm doesn't sound very romantic.
But I guess no one has to know the flavor names.

DARLA

I agree!
I focus less on the names and more on the flavor.
They are very popular cakes…
Like my other clients have loved them.
Is Sebastian supposed to come today also Jenny?

JENNY

Umm yaa…He said he would.
I'll text him!

(JENNY texts him.)

No response!
Haha such a popular one!
Sure he's texting all his bros…
Sure he'll be here soon!

DARLA

Ok sounds good.
Let's try "Fuck the Patriarchy" Vanilla!

(They all try the vanilla cake.)

CASSANDRA

Hmm it's ok.
Like I can taste the feminist rage in the icing
But I'm not sure how I feel about that.

JENNY

Also not sure if it's enough sugar
For me.

MOM

Mm this is the best part of the wedding.
I still think about my wedding cake.
It was shaped like a life-size mermaid
And was coconut.
After the wedding was over I ate so much
And your father got mad
At me.
Said I would get too fat to be married to.

DARLA

Wow a life-sized mermaid sounds so whimsical!

CASSANDRA

Yaaa wow.

MOM

My wedding was very very expensive.
My parents had to move out of their house for a bit
To afford it.
I think the vanilla's pretty good.
Vanilla is classic.

JENNY

I dunno
Isn't vanilla a little too simplistic
Like I want to wow people
At the wedding.

CASSANDRA

You def will!

JENNY

I wonder if I could get unicorn frappe cake,
Like with blue and pink swirls.

DARLA

I don't think frappes can be transfused into flavors though...

MOM

Also cakes tend to be one color.
Maybe if it was New York or something...
You could.

JENNY

Kkkkkkkk

MOM

Oh youth!
If I could, I would go back and do it all again,
Just to taste that cake again.

CASSANDRA

Yass I am so here for some cake.

JENNY

How's stuff with dad?

MOM

It's ok.
He got mad at me today
because I said I was meeting you.
I usually make him his lunch
Grind some bread from scratch and mix my own mustard,
Kinda amish friendly I know.

JENNY

I'm sorry he be pissed.

CASSANDRA

Yaa that sounds hard!

MOM

It's ok.
He's mad at me all the time so no worries.
I just try to ignore him,
Like everything he says
At all times.

JENNY

I can't believe one day I'll be married too!
We'll be two married ladies.

CASSANDRA

Cute!

DARLA

Let's try the "I Hate Men matcha!"

CASSANDRA

Omg I'm like too into matcha!
Like once as a performance art piece I like
Drank matcha for seventy hours straight
Like in a gallery
Like crying.
Like I had to go the hospital for a bit,
But it was so worth it.

(MOM eats the matcha cake intensely.)

MOM

This one tastes very trendy…
I think I… hate it?

CASSANDRA

It might be giving me PTSD….
Why did I think drinking so much matcha would be good for
my career!
No one even wrote about it…
Not even obscure bloggers
That cover matcha news.

JENNY

I don't really like it.
Kinda bitter.

DARLA

Sounds like a no!
Let's try the Lemon!

MOM

Mmmm tastes so sweet and old fashioned.

CASSANDRA

Ya feeling it.

JENNY

I hate lemon.
But Sebastian likesss lemon…
I didn't know wedding planning would be this hard.

DARLA

Good thing you have Darla at your service!

JENNY

Sebastian really should be here soon!
He loves cake a lot!

MOM

Sounds great!

DARLA

Looking forward to seeing him!

(MOM and JENNY eat the cake intensely.)

MOM

You're gunna be so happy Jenny.
Being married.
Being a wife.
Grinding mustard from scratch.
Cleaning his shoes for hours
While he's watching baseball.
Appealing to the male gaze.
Soo so happy.

CASSANDRA

Ya it's so exciting!
I can't believe you little Jenny
Will be a wife.
You're gunna feel so different.

DARLA

She really is!

JENNY

Uh huh…
Ugh I'm really upset-
Tomorrow's like the last day of the unicorn frappe…
Not that I care… just like
Putting it out there.

MOM

Too much coffee isn't good for you Jenny.

JENNY

Too much coffee isn't good for yo face?

MOM

Hunhh??

JENNY

I hate all these cakes so much…
I want to like throw them off a bridge,
To like throw them at ugly babies,
To like use them as sexy concrete.
They taste too feminist
To be served at a wedding…
Just nothing is what I want at alllll
Wahhhhhh

(Everyone looks traumatized.)

CASSANDRA

It'll be ok Jenny!

11.Oh Unicorn Frappe, what are you doing to me boi?

*(JENNY and SEBASTIAN's home. JENNY calls
SEBASTIAN.)*

JENNY

Hey baby mouse party
Are you coming home soon?

SEBASTIAN

No I'm shopping
For this lawyer beach thing.

JENNY

Oh kkkkkkk
When will you be back?

SEBASTIAN

I dunno…
Not sure
There's the wannabe lawyer beach getaway trip
That starts tonight
And lasts all weekend

JENNY

Ok I just…
I'm having a really hard time.
I keep seeing like dancing unicorns
And right now there's like a magic bowl of gold
Dancing and waving at me…
And I had such a bad day.
Cassandra like freaked at me cause she said
I drink too many unicorn frappes
And like can't function as a chick
But like she's not engaged- she doesn't get it.

SEBASTIAN

She probably was just trying to help

JENNY

Ya you're right,
Help is an important concept.
Ugh I feel a little dizzy,
Is it weird that a rainbow is trying to hug me,
Ugh I don't want to
Also they're fricking gone like forever,
Like they were ma bff
And now it's just like me.

SEBASTIAN

Hun, are you ok?

JENNY

I've just been drinking all these unicorn frappes..
But that's like normal and stuff
Cause Like I'm under pressure
And they like want to be drank so much cause like
They look like a sexy homoerotic 7th grade slumber party
With tie-dyeing
And they taste like childhood dreams like
Being something like an astronaut and
Like we're getting married so soon
Like legal documents like us signing and
(I love youuu)

SEBASTIAN

I know you do…

JENNY

Is it weird I can't feel my legs?

SEBASTIAN

It's probs just stress,
You've been working so hard.
Like your body is probably just being a little sensitive
To all the caffeine.

JENNY

Do you think about me? Like
At night,
Like when you're lonely,
Like when you're at a wannabe lawyer conference
At a non-disclosed location,
Do you like think about my hands and stuff
and how they smell like
Almond cause I grind almonds

JENNY (cont)
When I can't sleep, it might be a compulsive thing?
And like how sometimes my laugh is so delicate
it sounds like
A fairy princess?

SEBASTIAN
Course I think about you.
I think lots of thoughts
I think about my childhood,
Like playing with toy firetrucks
On my brothers face when he was sleeping
And like about eating marshmallows slowly,
And I think about
Whether it would be cooler
To die while acting in a nine hour play
And someone stabbed me onstage or
Like being attacked by hot chicks.
Probs the second one.

JENNY
But what do you think about mee?

SEBASTIAN
Umm it's hard to describe or
Remember...
Probably like your table manners and stuff...

JENNY
I do have some good etiquette training
Is it weird the floor has become
The ceiling?
Like usually things stay in like one place...
But now they're like not

SEBASTIAN
I think you're thinking too much.

JENNY

Ugh the unicorn frappe was like too good
For this earth.
And I was the lucky lady
Who was lucky enough to savor
Them in ma mouth
In their limited time on this planet.
And now they're gone.

SEBASTIAN

Jenny, everything will be ok.
It's just a drink.
Sounds like you were going a little overboard with them
anyway
So this is probably a good thing.

JENNY

It's not just a drink,
It's like a way of life, a calling,
A siren song whispered into a seashell,
My subconscious assembled into
Drink form.

SEBASTIAN

I should probs go soon.
We're all getting in this big party bus
To go the beach.

JENNY

Kkkkk I just…
Could you come back to the house right now?
I just don't want to be alone.

SEBASTIAN

I don't think so...
This is just gunna be a good networking opp for me.
I'm sorry.
I'll be back in a week
And I'll be there for you as much as you need.

JENNY

Kkkkk

SEBASTIAN

Ooo the reception's cutting out. I'll see you later Jenny.
Maybe spend a little less time here?

(SEBASTIAN hangs up.)

JENNY

He's gone...
And yet he's still hot...
Life is so weird.

*(JENNY takes some unicorn frappe cups out
from under her bed and starts cradling them.)*

JENNY

Oh unicorn frappe,
Your sweet cream feels so sweet against me,
And you're so rainbow-y and bright, like so free!
I wish I could be that free (why aren't I that freee?)
And when I touch you, you melt against me,
And that's cool,
Like literally cool.
And sometimes,
Sometimes late at night I wake up
And I lament your fate Unicorn Frappe
Cause you just so misunderstood,

Like people think you're too sweet
Or taste like lava or like drunken kindergarten,
But I don't think those things!
I think you're too beautiful to exist,
Like I think if I could touch you you'd disappear like
Like a figment of my imagination,
Like too good for this world,
And I wish you were served every day of the year,
But I get you're supposed to be a novelty,
But you're no novelty to me babez,
You are everything.
And some people don't like to have dreams,
They just like to sleep and see black
But I like to go to sleep and see you
Over and over and if I had my way,
I'd become a coffee drink maker,
A barista,
So I could make you every day,
Just so you could pop in my mouth every day,
I don't know what I'd do without you,
I don't know how I'd be without you.

12.Oh Unicorn Frappe comfort me cause ma Fiancé is MIA and you are but gone as well you little sugar hottie of the even!

(JENNY is in her room staring at her unicorn frappe cups. The PRINCE appears.)

JENNY

They're like gone and stuff,
They like stopped serving them.
Like one second, they were so hip
People from all over the world OD'd on their greatness,
And now suddenly they just disappeared.

JENNY (cont)

Like what am I supposed to do?

PRINCE

It's ok Jenny,
I can make you some more.
I legit sleep in a unicorn frappe moat and stuff,
They're everywhere.

JENNY

Omigod thank you!

(PRINCE gives JENNY an extra special unicorn
frappe.)

So does that mean I can only get them
when you're here?

PRINCE

I suppose so.
You been thinking about
princes lately?
And like royal family configurations

JENNY

No
Course not
I been thinking about my fiancé...
Been watching these home vids of him,
You know when he was six he held a real live duck
At his friends b-day party!
How cute right?
Imagine little Sebastian hugging
a duck!

PRINCE

Sounds cute...

JENNY

It was! He loved ducks...
Now I'm not so sure what he loves...
Hopefully ME-HAHAHHA
We're getting married in 2 weeks so he better
Your coat looks so shiny,
Like I wish normal men dressed like you.
Like embodied shiny-ness with their bods

PRINCE

They can if they want,
If they have good taste...
So you think I possess good taste?

JENNY

Ya... ya I do.

PRINCE

Do you like that I'm single?

JENNY

Ya... um it's nice to be like unattached and stuff

PRINCE

Do you like that all I can think about is
Kissing you?
I can't stop thinking about you Jenny,
Your sexy manic laugh,
Your sheer feminine optimism.

JENNY

But I'm supposed to get married...
I'm in love with an actual man.

PRINCE

I don't think he loves you though...

JENNY

Course he does…
He fricking proposed to me!
He put a ring in my ice cream
And I almost choked on it
But it was a fricking adorable moment.

PRINCE

He's never around! He comes and
Just goes,
And doesn't care how you feel about it.
I'm always here for you Jenny, aren't I??
he barely cares about your feelings.

JENNY

But I love him,
Isn't that all that matters in a relationship??
All the guys I dated before
Acted like sand paper,
Like boring AF,
And like they wanted to be with me and stuff but like
Kissing them felt like
Kissing a grocery bag
And when Seb talks to me
It's amazing, like I try to write everything down
Cause I wanna ghost write his autobiography one dayyyyy

PRINCE

I have something big to ask you Jenny.

JENNY

Yaaaa??

PRINCE

Will you run away with me?
I want to take you somewhere special,
Somewhere where gumdrops sprout off trees
And baby alligators swim in moats of unicorn frappes
And there are lots of unicorns and they will
All know your name!
And everyday is so sunny your fingers feel sticky
And you just are so so happy all the time.
And no one forgets to come home
Or forgets you're getting married-
Everywhere is just sugar and just happy
And just pink and just perfect.

JENNY

Oo that does sound fun!

PRINCE

Is that a yes??

JENNY

But if I go,
Will I see my family and friends again??

PRINCE

…
Ya!

JENNY

You really do look like him in the right light.

PRINCE

I'm sure not…

JENNY

But that's a really big decision
Cause like I an engaged lady and stuff.
Can I think about it?
Maybe I'll ask him to play the game of Life?
That olden times board game!
That would be symbolic!

PRINCE

Just let me know.
Wanna makeout?

JENNY

kkkkkkk

(They makeout.)

13. Oh Unicorn Frappe, do men still like board games?

*(We are at JENNY and SEBASTIAN's house.
JENNY calls SEBASTIAN.)*

JENNY

Hey, can you um come over in an hour-
I really wanna play the board game Life?
It's like when you create this whole life
And have kids and work at a bank
And it's like supa romantic.

SEBASTIAN

Oh um I have this SAT tutoring
Themed ice-cream scooping contest.

JENNY

We just haven't had any like
Couple time
And it's all a lot.

SEBASTIAN

I can try to be there in an hour.

JENNY

Thank you Seb!
Wow, you're such a romantic-
I hope they make a Disney movie
Inspired by you and your hotness!

(SEBASTIAN hangs up. JENNY looks at the
phone intensely. She then calls CASSANDRA.)

JENNY

Hey um, I don't know what's going on with Seb and I.

CASSANDRA

Ya??

JENNY

I can't tell if he loves me-
Or maybe I just don't know what love is!
But I invited him over to play a board game tonight
And I thought that could like solve all our
Problems and stuff
Like be so nice and stuff.

CASSANDRA

I don't think you playing a board game with him
Will make your issues go away.
I just feel like all he cares about is work.
Like you deserve someone who puts you
First.

CASSANDRA (cont)
Like I once dated a dude
Who wrote a seventy page long
Poem about ma hair-
Like that's what you deserve!

JENNY
I bet he'll like show up and stuff,
Cause he loves board games and stuff
And like soon we'll be a family
And have little mini kids
With glasses and big dreams-
Maybe it's just the wedding planning
That's driving me a little crazy.

CASSANDRA
Ya planning be stressful.

JENNY
Ok I should go! I want to set everything up
For when he comes
And look more physically attractive!

14. Oh Unicorn Frappe, bring me to ma happily ever after!

> *(At Jenny and Sebastian's home. JENNY is by herself waiting. SEBASTIAN enters.)*

JENNY
Hey…

SEBASTIAN
Ahh I'm sorry I'm late-
The mint chocolate chip SAT themed ice-cream
Was so good I could not stop enjoying!

JENNY

Your excuse is you were eating ice-cream??

SEBASTIAN

It was good…

JENNY

I wanted us to play
the board game Life,
Which was cute
a cute suggestion cause likeee
It's a metaphor for our future life!
I've been waiting for five hours…

SEBASTIAN

Well let's play it now!

JENNY

No, now I out of the mood.

SEBASTIAN

Kkkkk I can go, have more work to do anyway.

JENNY

It seems like the only thing you care about is work…

SEBASTIAN

Well that's your interpretation!

JENNY

But it seems like
it's the truth…

SEBASTIAN

We can play Life next week ok!
I should be free next Tuesday between 3 and 3:30pm.
You getting excited for our wedding?!!
Only like 9 months away!!!

JENNY

NO SEB!
No I'm not excited for our wedding!
Cause we don't even talk anymore cause you're always
M.I.A
And also ya dumped
Cause clearly you don't care enough about me
To make space for me in your life.

SEBASTIAN

I don't get it…

JENNY

Oh please don't die of a broken heart Seb,
Cause I couldn't bare it…
I don't want this either sweet Seb!
I just met
someone else.

SEBASTIAN

What? Who is he?

JENNY

He is but a humble member of the royal family…
And he wants to make me a princess…

SEBASTIAN

What country is he from?
Like what royal family?

JENNY

A hot country ok.
Don't laugh at me Sebastian! I'm happy now.
I'm not gunna live this fake life with you,
I'm gunna live a real life with him.

SEBASTIAN

What's his name?

JENNY

Huh?

SEBASTIAN

Does he have a name?

JENNY

Uhh Prince...

SEBASTIAN

He's a prince named Prince?

JENNY
What??
His parents I guess were literal ok...

SEBASTIAN

Does this guy even exist?

JENNY

Yes he exists,
He is but as real as you or I!
If I hit him, he falls!
If I throw him down an elevator shaft, he would
But bump a knee.

SEBASTIAN

That sounds kinda dangerous...

JENNY

Well maybe the love you have given to me
Is dangerous!!
Cause it is not constant,
It appears and disappears like
A sexy deadbeat dad.

SEBASTIAN

I just was excited for my tux,
Was gunna make my biceps look really good.

JENNY

Did you ever even love me at all?

SEBASTIAN

I really thought this was all going to happen,
Like the wedding and stuff and everything.

JENNY

Why are you making this so harddd Seb!!
Why so hardddd!!!

(JENNY is convulsing in agony.)

SEBASTIAN

(I think I should go,
This is a lot,
I need some wings.)

(SEBASTIAN leaves, JENNY doesn't notice.)

JENNY

I wish your love was wings
Not edible manly ones, but actual wings
 that could transport me away from this!

I wish you had strong enough wings to carry
Our relationship?
But you DO NOT!
This is over Seb!
This is over cause you never come home when you say you
do…
Cause you seem more turned on by the SATs
Then you do by me,
This is over cause you don't appreciate the beauty
That is
The unicorn frappe
Aka ma BFF,
This is over cause you don't appreciate beauty as a
CONCEPT
And also the beauty that is ma HEART
I thought a proposal from a real live man
Meant something,
Guess I was wrong,
But I found love Sebastian!
I found love in a hopeless place!
And dance break,
Fuck this speech sucks.
Wait… where did you go?
You just left…
But you didn't hear that big speech…
And I practiced for like four hours!
NOT COOL SEB!
It was so beautiful, like youtube video worthy…
And I was just about to launch into the
spoken word section that was
especially
Poignant :(

       (PRINCE appears out of the sky with Pecan
       Pie.)

PRINCE

How did it go?

JENNY

Awful.
He was so upset,
He like freaked out,
Never seen him that upset,
It was like Shakespearean level angst.
Didn't know men could feel that much.

PRINCE

Well I can relate,
Losing you sounds like the worst thing that could ever
Ever ever ever ever ever ever ever ever ever
Happen.

JENNY

Thnkssss
I dunno, I just didn't think it would hurt this muchhh.
Like letting him go.
He just looked so sad and stuff,
Like we had a life planned,
And great gift bags for all our wedding guests,
with pics of us in bathing suits
and now I have nothing.

PRINCE

You have me,
Me and Pecan Pie.

JENNY

Kkkkkkk

PRINCE

Just come with me Jenny.

JENNY

But I'm scared…
What if Sebastian will really love me,
I just should have give him an extra week or something
Or like some very persuasive
Couple's counseling DVDs?

PRINCE

It's not gunna happen Jenny.
Let's just go away.
Here's a unicorn frappe for you to drink
on the ride.

JENNY

Kkkkkk thanks

PRINCE

There's no need for you here.

JENNY

Kkkkk
Ok I'll go.

JENNY

It goes so fast doesn't it,
it goes so fast.
We don't have time to just look at one another.
Goodbye fair world! I shall miss you!

Epilogue- No More Unicorn Frappes

> *(We are at SEBASTIAN and JENNY's home.*
> *DARLA calls SEBASTIAN.)*

DARLA

Hi Sebastian,
I was just calling to check in
About my deposit.

SEBASTIAN

Oh of course!
Thank you so much for all the work you put
Into the wedding.

DARLA

Yes, well I did put in months' worth of time
So that will be fifty thousand dollars,
You see I have been working all weekend
On a glow in the dark unicorn for your
Photo booth
And my hands hurt so much I could barely dial the phone.

SEBASTIAN

Uh huh…

DARLA

So what happened between you two anyway?

SEBASTIAN

She dumped me.
It's complicated…
I think she thought I focused too much on work.

DARLA

I can see that.
Like you barely showed up at any wedding planning
meetings,
That's a rarity.
So about the money-
Hard cash would be great-

SEBASTIAN

Have a good day Darla byeeeee!

(SEBASTIAN hangs up. Phone rings again- it's from CASSANDRA.)

CASSANDRA

Hi, Sebastian??
Have you seen Jenny?
Like I heard the wedding was off…
But I haven't seen her since she posted that on facebook.
So what happened??
Did you dump her?
Cause you were very lucky to be with her,
She's such a friendly gal.

SEBASTIAN

No um, she um dumped me.
She said I focused too much on work

CASSANDRA

Well you were a pretty awful fiancé
Like just so into the SATs like all the time
So I get that.

SEBASTIAN

Um ok.

CASSANDRA

Why hasn't she contacted me?

SEBASTIAN

I don't know…

CASSANDRA

Did she like flee the state or something?

SEBASTIAN

We haven't talked since the breakup

CASSANDRA

Do you even know if she's ok???

SEBASTIAN

I'm sure she's fine…

CASSANDRA

She loved you a lot you know…

SEBASTIAN

Ya I know…

CASSANDRA

I'm gunna try to find her ok…
And I'll let you know when I do…
You're a jerk you know?
Like you could have tried a little harder?

SEBASTIAN

I don't know what you're talking about.

*(SEBASTIAN hangs up. MOM calls
SEBASTIAN.)*

MOM

Hey Sebastian…
I'm sorry to bother you.
I was just coming to see if Jenny was here.
Was hoping maybe you two got back together??

SEBASTIAN

No..we haven't.
And I haven't seen her in a bit.

MOM

I've never seen her feel the way about a man
She felt about you.

SEBASTIAN

It's fine.
It's probably for the best.
I'm pretty busy with work and she was acting
All weird and stuff...
That's not too hot from a male perspective.

MOM

Yeah I totally get that.
Will you let me know if you hear from her?
She usually doesn't go this long
Without talking to me.
Did she tell you where she was going?

SEBASTIAN

She said somewhere prettier.
She said somewhere where the sky
Explodes blue and pink confetti every two minutes
She said somewhere where men actually like you.

MOM

That sounds like a nice place.

SEBASTIAN

I think so too.

END OF PLAY